Hang On To Hope

A MEMOIR OF STRUGGLE, FAITH AND FIGHT TO KEEP HOPE IN THE FACE OF ADVERSITY

BY: CANDY BERTRAND

. . . .

Brian,

I pray that you find hope in The Great Hope!

We are praying for your healing and that this season brings the best fruit that God has for you and your family.

— Candy Bertrand

Acknowledgment

This story of hope would never be possible without my Creator because he never left my side even in my time of doubt. He is the True Healer of our family and life would not be worth living without him.

To my husband James. You have all my love and admiration. You are my steadiness in the storm and my peace in the chaos. Thank you for always being ready to lock arms with me and fight with me so that we come out stronger on the other side. You are mine and I am yours, always and forever.

To our children, Justin, Hali, Jude, Brayden and Braylynn, I may have only birthed one of you, but each of you has engraved your own unique places into my heart in ways that can never be erased, and the amount of love I have for all of you remains forever. Thank you for allowing me the space to love you.

To my girls, my squad and my ladies who stick closer than sisters, you have impacted my life by staying in the trenches with me through the storms and by celebrating with me while riding the rainbows. Your encouragement, your love, your words of wisdom and your strength for me have taught me what true friendship is all about. Your friendships will forever be rooted in my heart.

To all of you who prayed and supported us on our journey through the hardest year of our lives, you will never know the impact you had on us and how you helped lift us through the journey. You are the epitome of what God's love looks like through his people. Keep doing what you do so that others may feel your love the way we have.

To all the medical staff at Women's & Children's Hospital in Lafayette and Children's Hospital in New Orleans who cared for Braylynn and sometimes us, thank you for caring for our girl and helping her to live. We are forever indebted to you for your time and care to ensure her healing.

Thank you Hogs For a Cause Foundation for providing our family and families like ours a place to rest and recuperate while we helped our child heal.

Preface

In my world, the definition of hope means believing we will see something good occur out of an unfortunate circumstance we are facing.

When God placed this idea of writing a book on my heart I thought to myself, "Who would want to read a book by a tactless, tempered and tired wife and biological-co-adoptive mother of five?" God must have someone in mind who needs to read the words on these pages so that my hope becomes their hope, too.

Since this book is God's idea I am writing our story out of obedience to him, and I believe hope will become a part of your journey as it has ours. Our story is a story of a family continuing to hang on to hope through pain, despair and the unknown. My prayer is that our story brings you to know The Great Hope in your situation. I hope you enjoy walking into the pages of a recent season in my life.

Hang on to Hope

Chapter One
WANTING TO ADOPT

. . . .

James and I began our love story in the summer of 2000. We were working in retail together, and because we had one mutual thing in common, we were divorced, we became friends. Neither of us was seeking out a second marriage, or more children because we had different goals in life, but God was seeking it out for us, and we were married May 12, 2001.

James had two older children, Justin and Hali, and I had Jude, a baby at the time, who were all from our previous marriages. Since all of our children lived with us the majority of the time, we decided that we would not have any more children together: parenting three children on an almost full-time basis and having full-time jobs was enough for us. Or so we thought.

In 2005 as we sat in church listening to the devastating needs of those who suffered through Hurricane Katrina, our pastor said, "There are babies who need mothers and fathers because they lost their parents during the hurricane." I looked at our pastor on the stage as he continued to share the story of babies who needed parents, and I had an involuntary tug in my heart to mother and love on at least one of those babies that needed a momma and a daddy.

When I mentioned the idea of adopting to James, the answer was an immediate, "No." He said, "We are having too much difficulty raising the children we have, and we do not need to bring any more children into this family," and I agreed. For the following ten years as two of our children grew and left home and the other one prepared to leave for college, I still desired to mother at least one more child. Thus continued the hope in my heart of being a mother at least once more.

Some years later our church partnered with Department of Children and Family Services (DCFS) and had an event known as the Heart Gallery, where pictures of local children who were available for adoption were displayed in the church foyer. That Sunday James and I listened as the outreach coordinator described the need for homes for our local children. The coordinator said if only one family in every church in Louisiana adopted just one child, there would no longer be any adoptable children in the DCFS system. I asked James a couple of times throughout the previous ten years if we could adopt a baby, and the answer continued to stay the same, "No." However, because I am persistent, I decided that I could explore the possibility of asking James one more time if he would be willing to adopt a child.

In James's defense, he is ten years older than I am and felt he was done raising children. We were almost empty nesters, which had me understanding his point of view, and I never held it against him for not wanting any more children. Nevertheless, unbeknownst to me, God was stirring something up in James. At one of our other church campuses he had been looking through displayed pictures of children at the Heart Gallery, and I was unaware that he had his eye on a photo of a teenage boy who he thought might be a fit for a family. I was pushing forty and James was nearing fifty, and in no way did I want to ask him to adopt a baby. Therefore, I thought a teenager would undoubtedly be a fit for us.

The Sunday of the Heart Gallery event, I took a paper with a picture and description of a teenage boy and brought it to James. I handed the paper with the boy's photo to him and said, "Would you pray about it? If you say no, I will understand, and I will never ask you again." To my surprise, he answered, "I was looking at this exact picture of this boy at the other campus!" We decided we would attend the next information class for foster and adoptive parents.

Shortly after James and I agreed to move forward with adoption, we brought all of our children together at our kitchen table and presented our desire to adopt. We explained to them everything that we knew, in our naïve-about-adoption minds, about what we thought bringing another child in the family would look like for us. At the time, we had one teenage son still at home and two grandchildren from our oldest daughter, who was at our house often, so our top priority was those underage children, and we wanted our adult children to be on board as well. James and I discussed the possibility of adoption with all three of our children and our son-in-law to be sure everyone agreed with our decision to bring another child into the family. Adopting is not an avenue we were willing to travel down without caution because we knew it would alter everyone's role in our family. Our older children would have another sibling, and our grandchildren would get less time and attention from their Poppy and GG. Adopting would have a significant impact on everyone involved. Fortunately, all of our children agreed on the adoption of another child.

James and I went through all the classes and settled on adopting a teenage boy. Every time we called about the status of an adoptable boy, we heard a plethora of issues that we did not have peace about. Because we had two grandchildren under the age of three who spent a lot of time at our house, we began to reconsider if we wanted to adopt a teenager. We prayed and we had hope that God was going to send the right child who would be the perfect fit for our family.

While we were searching for the child God wanted in our home, a family that we saw regularly at church was fostering an eight-year-old boy who was about to be freed for adoption. This little boy also had a six-year-old sister who was ill and lived in a separate home that cared for special needs children. Our home caseworker asked a few times if we would consider taking this particular eight-year-old boy and a six-year-old girl. Each time the family in our church and the caseworker asked us to consider taking the children, we gave them the same answer, "No," because the thought of taking in more than one child, a young child or an ill child had not even been on our radar.

James and I were almost empty nesters, were not comfortable having small children while knocking on the door of our next decade and were in total agreement that we did not want to consider a child who was ill. At that time we thought we might have been nearly too ill ourselves to take care of little children. Just joking, maybe, sort of.

I am sure you have heard the saying, "Tell God your plans, and he will laugh." Well, I am sure He was laughing hysterically over there in heaven because after each phone conversation with an adoption worker about finding a teenage boy we were losing hope. It seemed like we might not find a child who would be a perfect fit for our family. We started considering the two young children we were being asked to take in. Were we going crazy?

Yes, yes we were going crazy. James and I began to pray about those two, way-too-young-for-us children and decided that maybe two younger children would be a good thing, that they would fit right in with our grandchildren and they could all grow up together. James and I live our lives by faith, so we dove right on in and said, "Yes," to the boy and girl who were about to flip our life upside down, turn it around, knot it up and tie it in a bow as the perfect fit for our family.

Chapter Two
OUR NEW CHILDREN ARRIVE

••

Brayden, who was eight at the time, attended our church with the family who was fostering him, so he was the first child we considered adopting that James and I laid our eyes on in person. We went to watch Brayden play in the children's area of our church, and I remember thinking how beautiful his smile was as he played air hockey with another child, and right then and there I knew he was to be in our family. The next day I called our caseworker and scheduled a meeting day for us to officially meet Brayden and his sister Braylynn, who was six years old, on a Saturday at our home.

James and I remember distinctly the day they came to meet us. I was so nervous about them coming, and I felt like I was going to throw up. What the heck was I supposed to do with two little children who I never met? My friends know this secret about me, and now you are about to know it, too. I do not like working with little children from the age of five until they are about ten or eleven. Children that age who I am not familiar with intimidate me, and I am generously thankful for other people who love working with children that age. So there, you now know that I had no clue what to do with these two children, who God was throwing in our lives. So I figured we would have to wing it and that is what we did.

The morning Brayden and Braylynn were due to arrive at our home to meet us, I made chocolate chip muffins because you can win over any kid with sugar, and we waited. The feeling of the arrival was awkward because we did not know how they would respond to us, and yet, to our surprise, it was very uneventful. Brayden and Braylynn were brought to our home in separate vehicles. They were both very excited to see each other, and for the majority of the time they were visiting our home we let them play together because just being together was enough for them, and they could not care less that James and I were even around.

For the next few weeks we had weekend visits with Braylynn and Brayden, and I was able to get one last overseas trip in, living my best life, with my best girlfriends before my and James's lives came to an abrupt stop. Imagine in your mind hearing the tires of a vehicle coming to a screeching halt: then you can envision exactly what happened in the Bertrand home on June 25, 2015. That is the day our comfortable life as we knew it was officially behind us.

Having Brayden and Braylynn become our forever children was not as close or as easy as we were made to believe that it would be in the beginning. James and I had a lot of experiential learning through a journey we had never been on before. We spent the first two and a half years that Brayden and Braylynn lived with us in and out of court, taking them to parental visits with a biological parent, going to oncology appointments for Braylynn and taking both children to therapy.

There were days when James and I thought we might not be cut out for the job of adoptive parents because we were not equipped to handle the trauma both children had experienced during their first years of life. Through those two and a half years we hoped and prayed that they would be ours forever because we had all worked so hard on bonding and becoming comfortable as a family. It was time for them to become Bertrands.

Finally our hope became a reality, and on September 20, 2017 Brayden and Braylynn became Bertrands! We celebrated them forever becoming a part of our family surrounded by family and friends. From then on there has not been a day we felt like Brayden and Braylynn were not a part of our family. James and I recently had a conversation with Brayden and Braylynn, and all four of us came to the same conclusion: we do not feel like there was ever a time Brayden and Braylynn were not a part of our lives. That is how we know they were created perfectly as a part of this family.

Hang on to Hope

Chapter Three
A YEAR AND A HALF OF FREEDOM

....

In August 2013, at the age of four, Braylynn was diagnosed with Philadelphia Chromosome Positive Acute Lymphoblastic Leukemia (Ph+ Chromosome ALL), which is an aggressive cancer of the blood and very hard to cure. This season began with a long battle with her disease that would put her through rounds of chemotherapy, losing her beautiful curly hair, many long days in the hospital and separation from Brayden.

In June 2015 when Brayden and Braylynn came to live with us, Braylynn was still undergoing the maintenance phase of her cancer treatment, which meant she had to take oral chemo daily and receive IV outpatient chemo weekly or bi-weekly at her doctor's office or the hospital. Over the next two years, those treatments lessened.

Braylynn had not yet attended school because of her cancer when she came to us, and she was approaching seven years old, so we decided that we would go ahead and put her in school since the number of treatments she needed was decreasing and she was much more stable. Despite never being socialized in a setting of her peers, still having regular doctors appointments and experiencing the chaos of parental visits that placed her in turmoil each time, Braylynn caught on to her school work well and adapted much better than we anticipated.

Imagine being a young child who has a new family, still visits her old family, is dealing with a disease, needs to implement school and church and is trying to successfully navigate her challenging life. It ain't easy folks, and it was definitely not easy for her that first year in our home. The layers of experience that consumed her were challenging to overcome. However, she worked hard through consistent therapy and became quite a fearless young lady up to this point.

It was not easy for Brayden either, but he did not have the amount of layering trauma Braylynn did. It took him less time to overcome and push through the things that were holding him back. The most significant thing we noticed about Brayden was that he was not going to let his past determine his future. The joy that the Lord designed Brayden with has helped him overcome so much and has made him into the great young person he is today.

If you are not familiar with what happens when children are placed into foster care, then let me explain a little bit. Children who are ripped from the family they have always known, no matter if that family is healthy or not, are shaken to their core and experience trauma to their brain, body and souls. Most of the time children who enter foster care come from a family who has intentionally or unintentionally caused them to experience trauma, and without proper treatment and therapy children are not able to heal and walk in the freedom God has given them.

Brayden and Braylynn experienced quite a bit of trauma during the first years of life; it has been both James's and my honor to watch them put in hard work in order to flourish into the young people God created them to be.

We all continued to move on in our newfound freedom as a family and began to be healthy in our minds, bodies and spirits. Braylynn's Leukemia treatment was finally over in October 2016, and she was able to have her mediport, which helped her receive IV meds or have blood drawn during cancer treatments, removed from her chest. What a glorious day it was when she had her mediport removed! Now she was able to do all the things an average soon-to-be eight-year-old could do without worry.

Within the first three years Brayden and Braylynn lived with us we moved from the country to the city, they started a new school, they were making great friends, Braylynn was cancer free, both of them were making great strides in therapy and life was going so well. In the latter part of 2017 after what we thought had been a tumultuous time, both children had finally become a part of our family forever. What we had been hoping for had come to its grand conclusion. I mean 2018 could only be better, right?

Hang on to Hope

Chapter Four
IT WAS MORE THAN JUST A RELAPSE

. . . .

Wrong! 2018 began like poop and turned into an awful stomach virus with diarrhea. At this stage in our lives our family was living life as any well-bonded blended American family does, but when you are the parent to five children you are constantly hoping that they are all doing well. Rarely does that happen all in harmony, as you will see going forward.

Our third child, Jude, moved off to college, and he was living his best life, but this momma was still learning how to adjust to her new role as his parent. We had a bit of a rocky start at the beginning of 2018 as we—all right, mainly me—was learning how to be okay with our out-of-the-house college student's decisions. Jude and I had not been seeing eye-to-eye on some decisions we both made in regard to our adult-child relationship, and I had to relearn my momma boundaries. We made it through that scenario with some wisdom and came out of it mostly unscathed.

Our oldest daughter, Hali, and her husband, Trent, were building their little family of five, while she continued on her path to her second hip surgery, where she would need our help to care for two of her three children, who were all under the age of six at the time. James and I figured, "No biggie, Poppy and GG," as our grandchildren lovingly call us, "got this in the bag, too." Hali had had multiple surgeries before when we helped out for long periods of time during her recovery by keeping the grandkids, and we always got through it with an ample amount of rest and relaxation after those little ones went back home, of course.

Then there was our oldest son, Justin, who was still trying to find his footing in 2018, while Brayden and Braylynn were continuing to build their new lives as Bertrands. James and I knew 2018 started with some minor hiccups, but we had dealt with tougher things before and knew we could conquer those mountains because we could overcome anything as long as we were together.

Braylynn was also still seeing her oncologist every two months because, although her Leukemia treatment was over, the protocol for her particular disease required her to continue doctor visits for an additional five years. Her oncologist monitored her regularly, and each year her visits lessened by an extra month.

As James and I were conquering all the little battles that came our way, Braylynn's oncologist found that her white blood cell (WBC) count was extremely elevated during one of her final two-year checkups. She recently had a stomach virus, and we thought that might have caused the WBC to elevate, but to be cautious her oncologist wanted her to come back again in a few weeks. The next visit showed her WBC at a better level, so the doctor monitored it for another two months.

At the same time Justin, who was still trying to find his grounding in life, hit a very rough patch that threw him into a downward spiral. He felt as though his life had become hopeless and he did not know how to handle anything, not even moment by moment. Through the entire month of May, James and I walked on pins and needles morning, noon and night, not knowing where Justin's situation would carry him. Justin's battle was so sensitive that we told only a few of our trusted friends who could pray for him and for us, as we did our best to help walk him through this painful time. When this situation occurred, we decided to compose our family motto, Hang On To Hope, because in that battle all we could do was hope for another day with Justin. Little did we know that the battles at the beginning of 2018 were the start of an all-out war that would last through the year.

Finally at the end of May, Justin's situation began to improve, his life was getting more stable, and we could breathe a little as we still hung on to hope for him to become stronger and more grounded. However, only a few days later, as I sat in the oncology office for Braylynn's results and she sat out in the waiting area with the Child-Life Specialist, the oncologist gave me the news that Braylynn's cancer had indeed returned. I immediately called James to share the results, gathered myself so Braylynn would not see me distraught with emotion and walked to the nurse's desk to receive further instructions.

Braylynn's oncologist gave her the same diagnoses of Ph+ Chromosome ALL that she had initially. The instructions were to go home, get things in order, return to the hospital the next day and be prepared to stay for a week.

A week! What the what? Geez, we still had Brayden at home, James was in his busiest time of the year for work, I was in the middle of earning a degree for Biblical Counseling and our other children also needed our help. What were we to do? A sick child with extended hospital stays was not in the preplanned calendar I had made for the year, and I did not even have time to make a well thought out plan for what was to come. We might as well have scratched out every part of the itinerary on the 2018 calendar and wrote only the words "hang on to hope" on each day for the remaining seven months because that became nearly all we could do.

We had to go home to tell Brayden and Braylynn what was to come. I will never forget telling Brayden. We decided to inform him first so we could deal with his emotions and talk to him about being mature, supporting Braylynn and taking his place in the family by helping out wherever possible.

It is times like these that I am so thankful to be a believer in Jesus and have the Holy Spirit residing in me. Only when the Holy Spirit guides you, tough questions are answered in a way that brings peace to the heart. When James and I told Brayden that Braylynn's cancer returned, he cried and asked if she was going to die. "I do not know, but what I do know, is that she is living today and that is how we are going to live," I responded.

Then we told Braylynn. Her first question, as would be the thought of many tween girls was, "Am I going to lose my hair again?" She loved growing it out so much since the first time she had chemotherapy that she did not even like to have it trimmed. We told her yes, but that going through treatment this time would be much different from the last time she had Leukemia. We assured her that we would be there throughout the entire process and that no one would leave her as they had before. She took the news in stride and went on about her evening without any more questions. I assume, because she had dealt with regular doctors and hospital visits for so many years, that this was just another part of the routine for her, so she felt no reason to worry at this point.

During Braylynn's first cancer treatment, Brayden and Braylynn entered into foster care. Some people may view Braylynn having the disease in the first place as a curse, but her early diagnosis back in 2013 could have very well been the thing that put both of them on the right path. That part of their story I will leave for them to tell, should they chose to later in life.

We have had all of our other children go to the hospital at some point in their lives for minor surgery or illness, but NOTHING compares to the hospital stays we experienced during Braylynn's cancer relapse. These moments, my friends, are when you find out who truly cares for you and will walk with you through every step of the journey. The moment we started publicly sharing that Braylynn had relapsed, every single person we could think of stepped up to help in any way possible.

Braylynn's oncologist told us that, because of this relapse, her only option for a cure would be a stem cell transplant and that we should start the process of looking for a stem cell donor. I remember the day clearly. It was Braylynn's first week of treatment in the hospital, and my friend Ryan was visiting with her daughters. The oncologist began telling me a few things that we should expect moving forward and what we could assume would take place during her transplant. Then the doctor said, "You will have to be in New Orleans for at least one hundred days...."

I can still see Ryan standing to the left of me while the oncologist stood in front of me and at that moment, I could see the doctor's lips moving, but everything went silent. My mind went somewhere else at the thought of leaving our children, our grandchildren and our entire support system, which was so large we were never in want for anything. My mind was in a fog and I could not get my brain to comprehend the magnitude of what was going to take place. How in the world were we going to spend nearly four months away from everything that was familiar to us?

At that moment Braylynn's relapse hit me. I started to get resentful toward this disease, and my struggle to hang on to hope increased. However, I disciplined myself not to give up and purposely reminded myself daily to fight with and for Braylynn. I did not want the enemy to take what God had put together, so many mornings I would pray, journal and put on songs that uplifted us so that we could stay in fighting mode. We were going to fight our way through this, and I was determined we were going to win, even though at the time I did not know what winning would look like.

I began to reach out and find other people who had gone through stem cell transplants. Their stories encouraged our family as we journeyed through the unknown, and although we read stories of some who did not heal in this life, we were inspired by those who did. The stories of those who made it through allowed us to continue to hang on to hope.

For the next four months, we spent sixty-two out of one hundred and twelve days in the hospital with Braylynn, either for multiple days of chemotherapy or from her battling some kind of infection due to the chemo wiping out her immune system. That was not counting the weekly doctor visits for blood and platelet transfusions or check-ups that would sometimes last all day as an outpatient. Approximately a month after Braylynn started chemotherapy, she developed pneumonia and became septic, which put her in ICU for two weeks. We came very close to losing her. Braylynn's Leukemia treatment was only in its beginning stages, and I felt like we were heading into the abyss of this awful disease.

Staying in the hospital so long and coming close to losing Braylynn while trying to figure out our next steps gave us another opportunity to remind ourselves of our motto, hang on to hope.

As we began living this heart-wrenching and tiring season, we realized we were beyond indebted to the supportive friends who surrounded us. I do not know if you have your tribe, but let me be the one to tell you, if you have not found them, then find them. Build your tribe while you are living in your good times and be a good tribe member, so when you are in need that tribe will be there like melted marshmallows and chocolate in your graham cracker because they will stick to you and fill you with goodness like no one else will. James, Brayden, Braylynn and I were literally in want for nothing during this time, except for Braylynn's healing, of course.

Through those first four months of Braylynn's treatment in Lafayette, we had a plethora of people who would spend the night with Braylynn or stay a few hours with her to give us a break. People brought us food, mowed our grass, came to have lunch with us and some took Brayden to their home for however long we needed them to. Others would visit us to see how we were holding up, send us encouraging texts or whatever we needed; we received from people who loved us. No amount of love that we have in our bodies could ever repay what we received during our time of greatest need.

Hang on to Hope

Chapter Five
SURRENDERING AND THANKFULNESS

Even with all the people supporting us and my Creator's love, I felt my spirit becoming more and more bitter about this situation. I missed being able to hang out with my friends when I wanted, I missed the time I got alone with James without discussing Leukemia and I missed serving in the ministry. I became upset each time I had to tell our grandkids they could not come over because Braylynn could not be around people. I longed to have my comfortable life back.

I have walked with the Lord for most of my adult life, and I have gone through good and bad times like anyone else. However, having a child who is ill and not being able to control the outcome brings life to a whole new level, and it is genuinely hard to figure out how to navigate your feelings in it. Through my years of having a personal relationship with the Lord, I have disciplined myself to sit with him in prayer and allow him to heal a lot of internal, deep-seeded wounds. My relationship with the Lord has led me to read and learn his word. Reading His word helps me when hard times come and I know where to turn even when I do not feel like it, especially when life becomes uncomfortable.

As I felt the bitterness creep up, I knew what I had to do. In the past, when I felt bitter, I read my Bible, I journaled everything I felt to the Lord: he always faithfully shows me the way in times of lament. I began to journal to the Lord every angry and bitter feeling I had due to this season of life. Here is an excerpt from one of my journal entries on one of my first resentful days.

7/2/18-"Lord, I had a very comfortable life. You saw fit to disrupt it for whatever reason... Help me keep Your perspective in this situation. What is Your goal? What do You want us to do in this situation? I know I have surrendered myself to your will, and I need to walk through this with my hands open and waiting... Is there something in this season that You want me to embrace, learn or change?"

As expected, the Lord quickly brought me his perspective and showed me how he needed me to begin to view things. He reminded me of 1 Thessalonians 5:18, which tells us to give thanks in every situation because it is Christ's will for us. That verse immediately prompted me to begin journaling all the things I was thankful for. Here is the continuation of that day's journal entry as my perspective shifted toward thankfulness:

"...I am thankful for Jesus and his healing blood, the sacrifice he made for me and I am thankful for James because he is my #1 on earth, my rock and my foundation. I am thankful for our other children who are stable and healthy.

I am thankful for Jason and Stacey and the way You have created them in their joyfulness to take Brayden in any time we need and at a moments notice and I am thankful for all the people who walk with us and help us in any way we need."

A few years ago, I read a book that had a profound quote that said, "Seeds of bitterness cannot take root in a thankful heart." When my heart is filled with more gratitude than bitterness, I can focus on the fight at hand. After I wrote the journal entry focusing on what I was thankful for, I was able to shift from bitterness to gratitude, and I conquered the weeks ahead with joy and hope.

Soon after, I realized we needed to bring people with us along the journey so they could see we were still hanging on to hope through our pain and walking authentically in hope. We decided we would start sharing written posts and videos about our journey through social media. I would often add the hashtag #HangOnToHope.

James and I posted things during Braylynn's cancer journey that we thought would educate people so they could help other families in crisis. We posted videos about how people could practically help others in need, how Braylynn was doing or how people could donate stem cells or blood. We sometimes shared posts about what God was telling us during this difficult time.

Sharing this part of our lives helped me because it made me feel connected when I could not be around people. It helped us share our journey and show that there was hope no matter how hard the struggle was. It was not an easy decision to put most of our private business out there because, of course, I was afraid of judgment and gossip. As a momma who reads the mommy blogs and social media posts, I see so many judgments from others on how to care for children, which is something I am guilty of providing, and I was afraid that how we handled our journey with Braylynn would be criticized. However, I did it anyway, and we got encouraging responses from people who said they felt like they were on the journey with us and told us how much it encouraged them, which helped us feel like we were fulfilling our purpose in our vulnerability.

Sustaining my thankfulness was not an easy task and continuing to hang on to hope was a lot of hard work. The only way to keep either of those two in check was to surrender to the Lord regularly, which I did through prayer, reading my Bible, journaling and keeping it real when I spoke to my friends about how I was feeling so they could help me stay on my gratitude track.

Keeping gratitude seemed effortless for James because he has such a natural, intimate relationship with the Lord, which allows him to endure the toughest times with such hope and grace. James reminds me of a prophet named Elijah written about in the Old Testament of the Bible. Elijah had a close relationship with the Lord that allowed him to be confident and bold when he acted on the Lord's behalf. Elijah's relationship with the Lord was so intimate that he did not allow Elijah to die. The Lord took Elijah up to heaven on a chariot of fire. I often think because James has such an intimate relationship with the Lord that He will not even let James physically die like me; He'll probably take James up in the sky in a chariot of fire like he did Elijah. I hope to have such a natural faith like James one day.

There were times I still got so angry and depleted that I did not think I would endure Braylynn's cancer journey well. Here is another excerpt from my journal a couple of months later on the eve of what I knew was about to be another LONG outpatient day at the doctor's office.

9/7/18-Lord, I don't have enough fight in me anymore. I can't even pull it out from the depths of my soul. I'm zapped. I know you will and are fighting for me and our family, but I can't feel it. Please get us to New Orleans or miraculously heal Braylynn without the transplant. We are now in our fourth month of fighting full force for her, and we are looking at another 6-12 months of fighting. We need to see an end, and right now it feels like we're swimming in an ocean with no land or rescue boat in sight. It seems as if our only two options are to wait or drown. Only you can make the land or the rescue boat appear, Lord, and I am getting frustrated in the waiting. Nothing since we've begun the adoption process was easy with Brayden and Braylynn, Lord, NOTHING. Can you just get us to a place where the road becomes smooth for a while? I am tired of everything being a fight for the last three years. I am only made to fight for so long. My body, mind and spirit can't take anymore. Just heal Braylynn, God!

Even reading that painful but perspective-changing moment takes me back to a place of conviction in how I need to shift my view back to God's view regularly. I also realize that in hoping for Braylynn's healing, I had not yet set my eyes on the One who gave me hope. I had been focused on the doctor's prognosis, the children who did not live through their treatments, how we were going to endure the next year and the uncomfortable, unrelenting daily battles. A little perspective change from the Lord was all I needed. Now, let's see if I can hold that perspective while spending one hundred days away in total unfamiliarity. The real test...

Chapter Six
A DONOR IS FOUND

. . . .

Children's Hospital in New Orleans notified us around the end of September that the donor center had found a stem cell donor that matched Braylynn. They were willing to start the process immediately. We began traveling back and forth from Lafayette to New Orleans two to three times a week for a month for testing. The only way Braylynn could receive the stem cell transplant was if she stayed in remission, so she had to go through one last chemo treatment in Lafayette, which lasted for five days in the hospital.

On day five of her last round of chemo, we received the news that her transplant would take place on November 6th and that her admission to Children's Hospital in New Orleans would take place on October 28th, her tenth birthday.

As we neared the time of Braylynn's transplant, we talked to Brayden and Braylynn about the reality of a hundred days away and the possibility that the outcome could be different than we expected. James and I do not hide things or lie to our children because we want them to trust everything we say and do. We believe that if God puts something in front of our family, then we talk openly about it, tackle it head on, and—if necessary—make it age appropriate for our young children's understanding. This situation was no different. We openly talked about what would happen if Braylynn would die, about heaven, and how we are not promised tomorrow. We shared how we had hope for Braylynn's healing, but we also knew we needed to be realistic and prepare for the worst. Kind of like the adage, "prepare for the worst but hope for the best." We even told Brayden and Braylynn to be open with each other about anything they wished to say: we did not want them to have regrets about things left unsaid.

During one of our open talk times, James asked Braylynn, "What is the worst thing that could happen to you?" We thought she would say, "I could die," but not Braylynn. To our surprise, she responded with, "I could go to hell." We were astounded by her sheer focus on where her soul was going rather than what would happen to her body. Imagine if we all thought beyond death and thought solely about eternity.

Moving forward, with each open talk, we tried to concentrate not on death but on how our decisions would focus on the eternal. These talks were not easy, but they were necessary, and looking back on it now, I am glad we allowed Brayden and Braylynn to face reality, showed them how to put their trust in the Lord's hands and not live in fantasy land.

I am confident that allowing them to deal with the truth during Braylynn's cancer season will help them endure hard times as they get older.

If you have ever experienced what a patient goes through during a battle against cancer, then you know that with every chemo session the possibility of death is imminent. Chemotherapy is a poison injected into the patient's body to kill cancer, but it also kills healthy cells and leaves the body defenseless against infection and the person is susceptible to germs in the air, in food, on clothing, and in the bed. Every. Single. Germ is dangerous to a chemo patient. If one germ enters the body of a patient with a completely obliterated immune system, then that could mean the end of their life. We do not realize how much our bodies fight daily to protect us from all the germs in our environment. Knowing that information allowed us to prepare ourselves should Braylynn's outcome be different from what we wanted, but it also allowed us another opportunity to hang on to hope. We prayed and hoped that Braylynn's body would stay germ free as she continued through her treatments.

Braylynn's transplant doctor informed us that her stem cell transplant would include more substantial doses of chemo than she had ever received before. It would also include radiation, which she had never experienced. The transplant team gives you the worst-of-the-worst scenario, and I already knew others who had received stem cell transplants who did not receive their healing on this side of heaven. Again we chose to hang on to hope.

Because Braylynn had battled serious infections before and even been septic and close to death four months prior, we made sure she lived her best life in October when we were home in Lafayette.

We celebrated her tenth birthday with all of her friends and family. We went to theater plays and the movies, and we visited as many people as we could, all while traveling back and forth to New Orleans and enduring a five-day hospital stay for her last chemo treatment. We were surely tired, but you better believe we were happy to have filled those days with tons of fun and numerous visits with our friends and loved ones. Braylynn also enjoyed those days. Having all that fun and attention allowed her to focus on what she would come home to. It is funny how we humans try to live our best lives when we think there is a possibility that we do not have much time left.

I remember the last day we spent in Lafayette before leaving for our new temporary home in New Orleans. The first thing we did was go to church. I love our church. We had been a part of our church for over seventeen years, and our spiritual family was as close, and in some cases closer, than our physical family, which made it even harder to leave our home.

When our pastor, Gabriel Smith, who loved and supported us beyond measure, and our congregation prayed over Braylynn and our family, I thought, "This may be the very last time I stand in this church where Braylynn is a part of it. The next time we come back here, she may not even be alive." Boy, I was not hanging on to hope much that day. We were walking into the great unknown, and all I could see was adversity.

After church, we had a light-hearted lunch, and then James and Brayden drove in front of Braylynn and me. Both of our vehicles were bound for New Orleans and piled with one hundred days worth of belongings. On our drive to New Orleans, I received a phone call from my friend Lauren to check on me to see how I was handling leaving Lafayette.

During that phone conversation it truly hit me that we were leaving our beloved home and that it was not going to be a happy fun-filled vacation. We were only an hour into the drive, and I remember telling Lauren that I already missed our adult children and our grandkids so much. During that phone call I concluded that I was not emotionally ready for this part of the journey at all. I tried not to cry, but I could not hold it back, and I once again laid my feelings before the Lord as we continued to New Orleans. I did not feel the Lord, but of course, I knew he was there, probably sitting right next to me in the front seat, helping me to see the road clearly through the tears.

Hang on to Hope

Chapter Seven
ARRIVING IN NEW ORLEANS FOR 100 DAYS

· ·

The transplant team told us it would be a hundred days. They were wrong: it was more.

The week before Braylynn received her stem cell transplant she received multiple days of radiation and heavy doses of chemo. These procedures wiped out every cell in her bone marrow that was her own, preparing her body to receive the donor cells. The hope was that Braylynn's bone marrow would receive the donor's cells as its own.

There were a couple significant risks associated with Braylynn's stem cell transplant. There was a risk of infection due to the elimination of her immune system from radiation and chemotherapy. Braylynn could acquire GVHD (Graft versus Host Disease), causing her body to recognize the donor cells as foreign, fight them, and possibly reject them.

The one hundred day time period did not include the beginning stages of the process for the chemo and radiation treatments. It only included Braylynn's transplant day, time for the bone marrow to accept the donor cells and for her immune system to start rebuilding. There was no rushing the procedures of the body's recovery process unless the Lord proved otherwise.

The medical team begins to count the days before a stem cell transplant with negative numbers until transplant day: transplant day is considered day 0. I took a different strategy and began counting from day -109 beginning the day we arrived. I was counting the days until we could go home.

My dear friend Kelly gifted me a journal that included the most timely hand-written, encouraging notes to me. I journaled in that book nearly every day we were there because I did not want a single part of this journey to be wasted or forgotten. I wanted to learn everything the Lord had for me, and boy did I learn a lot. I learned about myself and how the Lord will never leave me, even in my doubt, as you will see as we journey on.

The first day we arrived at Children's Hospital in New Orleans, we got to work by wiping down everything immediately, and I mean Every. Single. Item. Little piece by little piece, with sanitizing cloths. Then we were told that when we were in the hospital room with Braylynn we had to wear gloves, a mask and shoe covers, even while we were sleeping. WHAT???!!! Talk about uncomfortable sleep.

Thankfully James almost always took the night shift, and I took the day shift. I will never be able to thank God enough for how he timed Braylynn's transplant so that James could be off of work and stay in New Orleans with us. If I had to be away from my husband, I would have had an even harder time: after God, James is my steadiness, and there is no journey on this earth I would want to take if I was not nestled by his side.

After the sanitization process and recovering from learning how we would sleep, we were presented with the next set of shocking restrictions. No one but Braylynn could eat or drink in her hospital room, and she could only eat certain types of food, prepared in specific ways, and she could only drink bottled water. Each item, of course, had to be wiped down before it entered her room. There was no running water in her hospital room because water from the pipes carries germs, which meant anytime James or I needed to use the toilet, we had to leave Braylynn's hospital room. Once we left the room, we had to take all of our hospital coverings off, get a key for the "Transplant Parents Only" bathroom, return the key, scrub up and put back on all the hospital garb again before we could re-enter into her room.

I avoided drinking a lot before I went to Braylynn's hospital room each morning so I would not have to go through all of that commotion to pee. Braylynn had a bedside toilet because she could never leave the room, so bathroom duty was convenient for her.

The first week in New Orleans was the hardest emotionally. James had to go back to Lafayette a few times, and I cried every time he left until he came back. I missed my other children and grandchildren so much. I journaled about how hard it was to want one child to be well while wanting my other children to be with me. Immediately my thoughts went into what I knew to do and had done in the months before this.

I began to make a list of things I was thankful for. I journaled about how grateful I was for our healthy children and about how thankful I was that God provided us a place to stay next door to the hospital.

Our tiny one-room occupancy next to the hospital where all three of us, and eventually, all four of us, lived was about the size of our bedroom at home. On the days we were together at the same time in our tiny room it felt even smaller than it was, but I reminded myself to always be thankful for it because it allowed us to rest, bathe and take a break from that hospital room when we needed to.

Our temporary home was in a place that housed twelve other families. We shared a kitchen, dining room and laundry area. The first week we were living in what was affectionately known as the Hog's House, I did not make the best impression on other mommas.

The first morning we woke up at the Hog's House, I threw another momma's Styrofoam coffee cup in the garbage, not knowing she was coming back to use it again. I messed up her morning, and I knew I had not left a good impression with her. I am a coffee lover, and I know how not having my morning coffee makes me feel, so I offered her my personal coffee mug. Then I put another momma in a tizzy because I put my food in the fridge in the place designated for her food, and she left me a note letting me know about it. I was cautious each day after to place my food in my designated area. I was zero for two in building any meaningful relationships with the people in our temporary home.

We all had to give each other some grace. I mean, trying to adjust to living with twelve other families who are also going through a crisis is hard. Some are not quite sure how to give grace in the midst of their turmoil, and that is understandable when you are in a difficult time. However, I made it my mission to befriend people by letting God send me those who needed a friend, which he did, and I had some delightful moments with other mommas like me. I eventually had some great conversations with the momma who I imposed on when I put my food in her area. Grace can open a lot of doors to meaningful relationships.

As the days went by I began missing my friends more and more. During our first week in New Orleans my beautiful friends, Amanda, Kelly, Lauren and Rhonda sent me a video message to lift my spirits, and I bawled the entire time. I felt like I was missing out on so much life that was happening while we were gone, but I was so happy they thought of me and took the time to cheer me up with that video.

My dear friend Ivette sent me off with one of the most beautiful treasures I received. It was a box with cards from all my girlfriends, in which they shared handwritten messages of encouragement, and little trinkets that would help me while I was away. Every day when I opened up a handwritten note, I felt like I was receiving a long-awaited gift. Every word made me feel adored by God and my friends, all of whom I valued so dearly.

My dearest friend who is like my sister, Cortney, checked on me nearly every day from her home on the other side of the world. Amanda, Rhonda or Lauren sent me a video chat every single day. I was never alone through this process, and it was one of the main things that kept me going while I was away from home.

Y'all, I cannot tell you how important it is to build your tribe while things are going good so that when you are desperate, they will be there for you when you need them most. The ladies who encouraged and supported me through my most challenging time are the sprinkles on my cupcake.

In addition to emotionally adjusting to this situation, we had to persevere through all of Braylynn's preparation procedures. For the first three days in the hospital Braylynn had to be transported by ambulance to another hospital for her radiation treatments. Braylynn had to be taken out of isolation, prepped for sterilization prior to travel and then sit entirely still for thirty-minute long radiation treatments. After the three days of radiation came the massive doses of chemo, which could not sit in her body for too long. She had to have a catheter for over a week, which allowed all chemo to drain out immediately from her urine. Braylynn's sheets had to be changed twice a day so that she would not lay in any of the chemo that leaked out of her skin. I am still in awe of the amount of poison that was injected into Braylynn's body and how she was able to live through it.

As the days went on, we started to see Braylynn decline physically. Her appetite and energy faded, so this momma devised a plan. Braylynn is our child who could stay focused on a screen all day if she was allowed. From my years of momma research, I know that too much screen time and not enough body movement can affect a child's brain, attention span and health. I wanted Braylynn to arrive on the other side of this disease stronger, not weaker. I devised a plan to get Braylynn moving in her brain and body.

Since I knew Braylynn loved staring at a screen for as long as possible, and one of our friends had recently purchased a tablet for her birthday, I knew the T.V. and tablet could be useful tools for helping her endure the transplant healing process. James and I fervently followed all the doctor's directions because we knew God did not bring her this far to only bring her this far, and we did not want to cause anything to go wrong, but I also knew it would not be suitable for Braylynn just to lay there and do nothing. Commence momma's plan.

I wrote a list of tasks Braylynn had to accomplish each day if she wanted to watch T.V. or play on her tablet. She had to eat, even if it was a little bit. She had to complete her schoolwork, exercise, brush her teeth, bathe and put special creams on her skin. I was determined that she would not feel sorry for herself and would take care of herself as much as she could since God was giving her this second chance at life. Let me tell you, Braylynn was ready for the daily challenges.

She took every task on like a champ, and even when she did not feel her best, she did it anyway. Each morning when I would trade out shifts with James, Braylynn would tell me all the tasks she had already completed for the day. She would say, "I'm doing what I can to get out of here." I was hopeful we would be released earlier than planned and for her prognosis.

It is fascinating how a little motivation can help a person to reach their reward. We were watching a fighter who had hope that God was going to heal her.

Chapter Eight
TRANSPLANT DAY

....

Transplant day finally arrived, and this was the day Braylynn would receive her second chance. I remember waiting until late afternoon for the donor cells to reach her room. It was a glorious moment when they brought that syringe full of donor cells into Braylynn's hospital room. It is not a fancy process. It is much like a blood transfusion, but to us, it was a new beginning. On November 6, 2018 at 3:30 pm, Braylynn received her new life; she would no longer be at the mercy of damaged cells that ravaged her body. As the stem cells made their way through the tube and into her body through her IV, I was blown away by the thought that someone gave their time and cells to provide Braylynn with an incredible gift.

That stem cell donor engaged in a selfless, genuine act of serving someone who will never be able to repay them. As the donor's cells flowed through Braylynn's body, her primary transplant doctor, who administered the cells, said, "There is still such good in the world."

That doctor's words were a great reminder to us that there is still so much good in the world. Through this good, God gives us little glimmers of hope in so many places. The challenging part is choosing to find the good wherever we can.

We used Facebook Live Streaming to video the transplant taking place to allow the people who supported Braylynn and our family along this journey to experience and celebrate the beginning of Braylynn's new life. As I look back I realize how brave we were for sharing that moment because we allowed people to see one of the most intimate pieces of Braylynn's treatment. I was overwhelmed with emotion and could barely talk in some moments: something could have gone wrong, or worse, she could not make it. But I am glad we allowed people in because those who watched our journey said it gave them hope and that they felt like they were on the journey with us.

After we watched the stem cells enter her body along with the rest of our social media viewers, all we had left to do was wait out the days to see if the stem cell transplant was indeed her cure.

The night of Braylynn's transplant our tribe blew us away once again. Our pastor, our friends, our family and people from our neighborhood gathered together in our home in Lafayette to worship the Lord for his provision for Braylynn and to continue to pray for her healing in the transplant process. James, Braylynn and I were able to join in the prayer time from Braylynn's hospital room via video. All three of us wept as we watched everyone gather in our home. We felt so cherished as all of those people provided our family with another layer of love and support.

I do not even know if all of those people who joined together in prayer for Braylynn and for us realized how they increased our hope by leaps and bounds as we moved forward through the toughest part of this process.

Y'all, I will say it again, find your tribe. When you do that tribe will never leave you in your time of need, regardless of the distance or circumstance.

Hang on to Hope

Chapter Nine
WAITING

....

One of the assisting doctors on the transplant team, whom I called in my journal "doubting doctor" because he always told us the worst that could happen, told us that days +3 and +4 would be the hardest of all for Braylynn. On the day the doctors told us about days +3 and +4, I journaled about how the week before the doctors also said that radiation week would be very hard on Braylynn, but it turned out not to be as hard as they predicted. Because Braylynn had done better than expected during the first week, we had hope that she would not feel as bad as the doctors anticipated.

During one of my daily video chats with my friend Amanda, I shared with her what the doctors told us about days +3 and +4 being hard on Braylynn. Amanda receives a lot of knowledge from the Lord and shares it with me. She suggested we rename days +3 and +4 to something more positive, so we did. Amanda told me that I needed to be sure to journal my experience as thoroughly as possible because I would write a book. But in my mind, I thought, "Nah, I won't write a book, I have no desire to write, nor do I speak or write eloquently enough for others to desire to read it, but I love journaling, so I'll keep doing that."

We renamed day +3 "Day of Joy." From that day forward, we decided we would rename each day that Braylynn was in the hospital to something positive. We even asked the medical staff to get involved and help us rename our days. Below is a list of the days we renamed.

Day +3: Day of Joy. We chose to live in joy this day.

Day +4: Day of Miracles. On this day Braylynn started running a fever, so we looked for miracles everywhere we could and believed that Braylynn was still in the middle of her miracle. We asked the nurses to share their miracle stories with us, and some nurses told us marvelous stories. I love hearing how wonderful God has been in people's lives.

Day +5: Day of Hope. God was showing off on this day. The doctors told us that by this day, most patients were on IV nutrition. But not Braylynn! Even though she struggled, she ate as much food as she could handle and drank supplemental drinks that helped boost her nutrition. The transplant team was amazed at how well she was doing physically through this process. Knowing how impressed the doctors were with her progress allowed us to hang on to hope. Our scripture for that day was Hebrews 6:11, which says, "But we long to see you passionately advance until the end and you find your hope fulfilled," (TPT). We were indeed ready for our hope to be fulfilled.

Day +6: Dripping with Confidence. The isolation was getting old, as was the mundane routine. Braylynn had been in isolation for sixteen days, and I needed some confidence that day. I journaled John 5:14, "And this is the confidence that we have toward him that if we ask anything according to his will, he hears us" (ESV). I told the Lord in my journal that I was confident he would continue to strengthen me. I am thankful he held me up with his strength.

Day +7: Day of Courage. Today we asked the staff to share with us stories of courage. We loved hearing their stories of other children who had gone through the same process as Braylynn—hearing their courageous stories encouraged us to get through this process as well. I journaled that day about how James was the epitome of courage because he stuck by us without ever thinking of himself through this whole process.

Day +8: Day of Renewal. Today we believed and prayed that God was renewing Braylynn's bone marrow, and we stood on Isaiah 40:3, which says, "But they who wait for the Lord shall renew their strength; they shall mount up with wings like eagles; they shall run and not be weary; they shall walk and not faint," (ESV).

Day +9: Day of Wellness. On this day we put a post on social media that included a picture of Braylynn's increasing immune system numbers. The picture included her Absolute Neutrophil Count (ANC) written on a dry erase board hanging on the wall. The ANC number was an indicator that her immune system was getting better.

"Wellness-an approach to healthcare that emphasizes preventing illness and prolonging life, as opposed to emphasizing treating diseases.

Every day we try to speak life. Although today is a slower day to see wellness, we believe it is there in Braylynn's body because there is no disease to treat.

See how the ANC is up to 4 from 0? That is way off from 500, where we want it to be, but the slightest increase to us shows the emphasis on her body wanting to prolong its life.

Today we are thankful for slight improvements because every slight improvement builds to big improvements.

As you can see from even the slightest improvement, wellness is happening."

Day +10: Day of Praise. Braylynn's immune system numbers had not yet changed at this point, but we decided to hang on the Word and praise Him anyway. "Because your steadfast love is better than life, my lips will praise you," Psalms 63:3 (ESV).

Day +11: Day of Learning. I believe we should always be students who learn from everything, everywhere and everyone. This day prompted us to start learning about something new. Braylynn and I chose pineapples, which are her favorite fruit, and avocados, which are one of my favorite foods.

Day +12: Day of Rest. Today we took things slow and did some Masgutova Neurosensorimotor Reflex Integration (MNRI) work so Braylynn could still get her body and brain work in but not overexert herself. My non-academic description of MNRI therapy is that it focuses on reflex and sensory integration for anyone who has experienced trauma. It helps people become what I call "unstuck" in their brain.

In the past we have used MNRI therapy for Braylynn and Brayden to help them overcome trauma and comprehend themselves better. It is the top trauma-based therapy that I have ever experienced. If you or someone you know has had any trauma in their life (haven't we all?) and needs healing in that area or is just feeling stuck, I highly recommend MNRI therapy. It has been so beneficial for our children and for us. You can find out more information at https://masgutovamethod.com/.

Day +13: Day of Conviction. Our friend Donald gave us this word, and it was perfect for this season. Here is a post from our social media page that day.

"Conviction: a fixed or firmly held belief.

Many months ago, when Braylynn found out she relapsed, her words were, 'If God is allowing me to walk through this, then I just have to get through it.' A dear friend gave us today's word of conviction, and it brought me back to that day Braylynn uttered those words because she has full conviction that God is in control of her healing process and that he has set everyone in her path to help her along the way."

'Now faith is the assurance of things hoped for, the conviction of things not seen,' Hebrews 11:1."

Day +14: Day of Commitment. We asked ourselves on this day, "What would happen if we did not stay committed to the process that God set before us?" "What if Jesus did not stay committed to the process of becoming our Savior?" "What if the doctors and scientist who learn about saving lives did not stay committed to the process?" "What if the nurse who worked with and cared for Braylynn did not stay committed to the process?" "What if James and I did not stay committed to the process of adopting?" "What if Braylynn's stem cell donor did not stay committed to the process of donating?"

None of these things were easy for anyone to stay committed to, especially Jesus. However, each person persisted in their struggle, and the reward for every person's commitment was the hope they gave to others. My question for you today would be, "What is God asking you to stay committed to so that you can see hope fulfilled the way many others have?"

Day +15: Day of Healing. Braylynn was not feeling well on this day. The doctors believed that she was not feeling well as a result of the healing process taking place in her body. That prompted us to go to the Word and pray.

When James and I want the Bible to come alive, we insert our names in relevant places and speak that scripture over us. On this day, we placed Braylynn's name in Mark 5:34 and believed she would heal. We wrote out, "And he said to her, 'Braylynn,' your faith has made you well; go in peace, and be healed of your disease."

Day +16: Day of Abundance. This day was Thanksgiving Day. We reminded ourselves that we were in total abundance of all we needed on this journey and wrote out everything that was plentiful in our lives. We had an abundance of housing, God's love through his people, care through Braylynn's medical team, food, traveling safely, health and healing for Braylynn. We actively thanked the Lord for all the abundance he provided us with because it nourished our souls.

It was also an especially happy day because we could have people visit our tiny room next door to the hospital, so one of our grandchildren got to stay with us for a few days. All of you who are grandparents know how happy that made us.

Day +17: Day of Bravery. We chose bravery because Braylynn consistently showed bravery throughout her last ten years of life. When she underwent medical procedures that she knew would hurt, she would recite, "Be brave, be brave, be brave...." Constantly reciting "Be brave" always reminded me to be brave in the site of pain or uncomfortable situations.

Day +18: Day of Transformation. Braylynn and I had a great discussion on this day about how her illness had transformed us. We never want to waste any season God puts before us, especially one of this nature, so we evaluated how God had transformed our hearts and mind.

I discussed how God helped me transform the way I view people, reevaluate all the tasks I had going on in life and how this season taught me to focus more on what was important, which was God and his people.

Braylynn said that God helped her transform to be more obedient. She did not want to get in trouble and be sick at the same time because that was too much. I think it is interesting how children think differently than adults do.

Day + 19: Day of Prayer. This day was tough because I had some emotional hurt I was dealing with and Braylynn started to run a fever. In times like that I try to turn the spotlight in a different direction and ask God to help me view the situation from his perspective so hurt or disappointment does not override the hope that we try to hang on to. This day led me once again to my journal and prayer time with the Lord, and as usual, my eyes shifted to God where my hope was.

Ephesians 1:16 says, "I have not stopped thanking God for you. I pray for you constantly." Instead of focusing on my hurt, I put my focus on prayer and gave many thanks that day for our medical team, all the people who supported us through our journey and to God who provided all of these things.

Day +20: Day of Laughter. This day was an absolute miracle that happened by the grace of God. Braylynn progressed so well that she was discharged from the hospital ten days earlier than expected! We decided to make our last day in isolation fun.

Anyone other than her medical team, James, or me, had to communicate with Braylynn through her hospital door window so she would not be exposed to germs. Joe & Joe, the hospital clowns, came by and played with Braylynn and told her jokes through her hospital door window. Braylynn and I told jokes, took pictures with funny props and then hightailed it out the doors of the hospital to our tiny one-room room next door at the Hog's House!

Here is a joke you can tell yourself to lift your spirits when you are in a bad mood. "Laughter is the best medicine… unless you have diarrhea." (You're welcome.)

As we left the isolation unit behind us, I could not help but think about all the things that got me through those lonely but reflective days in the hospital. Many things helped us get through isolation, including daily video chats, texts from friends, praying, journaling, helping Braylynn with daily tasks, and taking breaks at the Hog's House next door.

Our friends and family came to visit us, and those times made me feel like I was not forgotten. I will never forget how much comfort it brought me when our friends, Marty and Sheri, drove down to visit us in New Orleans. That was the day God solidified for me that we had not been forgotten, which I had been afraid of when we first found out we had to stay one hundred and thirty-four miles away for one hundred days from all the things and people we knew and loved.

Another sweet visit we had while in isolation was when our friend Melissa and her daughter Izzy came to visit Braylynn. They used window chalk to write messages, play games and draw with each other on each side of the hospital door window. My sister-in-law Sheila and her son also drove to New Orleans for a visit and played window games with Braylynn. I think Sheila had the most fun out of anyone else who visited with Braylynn at her window because she has a passionate heart for Braylynn. I know it may seem sad only to be able to talk or play through a hospital door window, but you take what you can get, and you find creative ways to have fun when you are in isolation for a month.

Having people play with Braylynn at her hospital door window helped her stay connected to the outside world because, although James and I could leave the hospital,

Braylynn was never allowed outside of her hospital room until she was discharged a month after her arrival.

I experienced precious moments each Sunday when my sweet, encouraging friend Rhonda, recorded through video chat the worship services at the church we attended together so I could experience our church that I missed so much.

Another one of our friends, Stacey, made it her purpose to visit us in New Orleans with her husband, Jason. She also brought along our other friends, the Goulas and Comeauxs, because she read, "Families who had to be away, needed people to come and visit to keep their spirits up." Having this group of people around that day did fill my spirit and brought warmth to the dreary winter filled with isolation.

I am so grateful that God surrounded us with such great friends during our isolation period. These are the types of people you want in your tribe, y'all. Get you some friends like these!

Hang on to Hope

Chapter Ten
FREEDOM...SORT OF

All four of us were finally all together in our tiny two-hundred-square-foot room. Being out of the controlled, germ-free environment of isolation was very stressful. Because Braylynn's immune system was still deficient and rebuilding, we had to stay close to the hospital for the next couple of months in case anything happened and we needed to get her to the ER quickly.

We had to be very cautious of germs everywhere we went. Our days were filled with reminding Brayden to remain germ-free at all times to protect his sister. Staying germ-free was next to impossible for a twelve-year-old boy and way too stressful for a mom and dad who are trying to keep their other child alive to stay on top of.

This part of the journey became very long because we spent every single weekday in the clinic for lab work, blood and platelet transfusions and IV medicine. All of these procedures would take hours and hours. There were days we spent eight to nine hours in the doctor's office. All I can say about that is, "Ugh," because being stuck in a dull white room with no windows, sitting in a tiny chair, without television for an entire workday (without the pay) can make a person stir crazy.

When we first left isolation, there were only two days where all four of us could be together in our tiny room before Braylynn was back in the hospital.

She started running a fever, and the doctors thought she was developing GVHD because Braylynn's body began to recognize that the donor cells were not hers. Her body interpreted those cells as foreign objects and began to attack. At this point, things got worrisome for us because we recalled all the things the transplant team told us could go wrong or be fatal. There can be different levels of GVHD. Level one is good because it affects mostly the skin, and the doctors like to see a level one because it also indicates the body is accepting the donor cells. Level two is moderate and affects certain organs but can be treated, and level three, well, I do not even want to write about level three because it is not something anyone would want to experience. The best outcome is for GVHD to stay at its lowest level. Thankfully Braylynn's GVHD stayed at a level one, but it was still not a fun process. She ran a fever for days, her skin was itching and burning, and it was outright uncomfortable.

One pleasant difference during this hospital stay was that Braylynn could have limited time with visitors as long as they were not sick and wore face masks. Braylynn's first visitors were her friends Olivia and Isabelle who stopped in for a couple of hours while they were in New Orleans for a sports tournament. My sister-in-law Sheila, who Braylynn adores, visited with her daughter and granddaughter. This time it was more enjoyable since they did not have to communicate through her hospital room door. It had been so long since Braylynn was able to interact closely with family and friends, so it was a sweet treat for her.

A not-so-pleasant difference during this hospital stay happened when we had to make a quick trip back to Lafayette to put one of our vehicles in the shop for repairs. Since Braylynn was under close watch with the nurses, the sitter I hired would be coming in and Braylynn's pain and fever were under control, we thought it would be the best time to make the quick trip to Lafayette before immediately returning to New Orleans.

Well, it was not the best time. I received an unpleasant phone call while driving over Lake Pontchartrain on my way to Lafayette. The doctor called me on my cell phone, and I could hear Braylynn screaming like never before. They were trying to conduct a skin biopsy to confirm that the skin GVHD was causing the fevers. They needed to cut a piece of her skin from her back, which required a shot to deaden the skin and she was refusing to have it done if I was not there.

Dear Lord in heaven, the screams that girl was letting out made me think they were holding her down with straps. I spent the next twenty minutes on the phone trying to calm her down so that they could give her the shot. Once they administered the shot she did not even realize it when they did the skin biopsy and was totally fine. I guess her usual mantra of, "Be brave, be brave…" had gone out the window that day. I realized that instead of enjoying the much-needed break for a few hours, I had to finish that trip as quickly as possible. Whew! Thank God that was over with, or so I thought.

As soon as we arrived at the mechanic shop we quickly parked the vehicle, dropped the keys off, and headed straight back to New Orleans to get back to Braylynn. Well, on the way back we received another phone call from another doctor telling us they started Braylynn on a new medication to help prevent an infection they believed she was getting, but it caused an anaphylactic reaction! If you are not aware of what an anaphylactic reaction is, it is a condition that occurs when a person has an allergic reaction to something. They can break out into a rash, develop hives, their throat can swell up and it can be fatal. Braylynn's reaction was almost fatal.

The doctors gave her epinephrine, Benadryl and another steroid. I could not believe after all the procedures Braylynn had gone through and all the poison that had been injected in her body over the last few months that we almost lost her to a medication that was supposed to help protect her from infection. Thank you, Jesus, that a nurse was there with her to monitor her and did not just start the medicine in her IV and leave the room. Had that nurse not been there, you would be reading a different version of this story.

James and I came to two conclusions at that time: that nurses are truly under-appreciated in the care they give and that until Braylynn had completely recovered one of us would always stay with her.

Around day +30, while Braylynn was still in the hospital for GVHD, the time came for her first bone marrow biopsy since the transplant. This test told us that there were no signs of Leukemia and no Ph+ Chromosome detected in her blood. What a nerve-racking time that was. During that time of waiting her GVHD improved, but she developed Cytomegalovirus (CMV). People who have received stem cell transplants commonly develop CMV. A healthy person could have the virus without knowing it because their immune system fights it, but for someone with a weakened immune system like Braylynn, CMV can be fatal if it is not caught early. Thankfully Braylynn's transplant doctor tests for CMV routinely and early, and the virus was found in her system with ample time to be treated with weekly, four hour-long IV medicine.

Guess what that meant? Two weeks after Braylynn was discharged from the hospital, she stayed at the doctor's office for extended day-cations of IV medicine to treat the CMV and to receive blood and platelet transfusions.

Some days James and I wished she would stay in the hospital until it was all over because at least there she was better protected from germs and we could take a break from the hospital room while the nurses kept an eye on Braylynn when she pressed that red call button. But in the doctor's office we were stuck in there for a solid, dreary day. No part of this was an easy or pleasant journey, folks.

We did, however, receive the best news ever during this hospital stay. Braylynn's bone marrow aspiration came back negative for Leukemia, negative for Ph+ Chromosome, and her blood work showed that she was one hundred percent donor cells! Braylynn being one hundred percent donor cells meant that the donor cells had engrafted into her bone marrow and was accepting the cells as her own. Braylynn's bone marrow was now starting to create its own cells from the donor cells. Hallelujah! Things were beginning to look bright, and we were hoping for the possibility of celebrating Christmas at home, even if it were just one day.

On Day +45 we were given permission to go home for Christmas, with a lot of protocols in place, and we had to go right back to New Orleans the day after, which meant we had to keep our reservations for our tiny one-room room next door. We were not only allowed to go home for Christmas, but we were released for four entire days because Braylynn was doing so well, and with Christmas on Tuesday, the doctor's office would be closed for four days. It was the heavenly day on earth I had imagined for a while! We were getting to spend at least one out of four days with all of our children and grandchildren. What more could a mom and dad and Poppy and GG ask for?

Apparently we were asking for a lot, because we were home in Lafayette for less than twenty-four hours when Braylynn started running a fever again, and we had to rush back to the hospital in New Orleans. It was not a pleasant trip, either. It was Christmas weekend on I-10, and traffic was backed up for hours. Me, the Nervous Nelly, prayed and prayed as we drove on the shoulder to get around the stand-still traffic and found alternate routes to get Braylynn to the ER as quickly as possible, and I sat through that drive full of disappointment because we had been so close to home yet oh-so far. On this ride I began a huge showdown with God and questioned how much longer I could hang on to hope.

Hang on to Hope

Chapter Eleven
THE BATTLE FOR HOPE

• •

Friend, I do not know how you face your disappointments, but I usually have a pity party, wrestle with God, he slaps me upside the head with his glorious insight and then I pull myself together and move on. Typically it does not take long, but this time was different. I was emotionally and spiritually weak, I was physically tired, I was tired of being disappointed and I was tired of having a little bit of hope dangled in front of my face to have it yanked away from me. I felt like the girl in the State Farm commercial, where the old man dangles a dollar from his fishing pole in front of the young girl's face teasing her, only to yank the dollar away from her. Disappointing her because the dollar she hoped for was so close but went away as quickly as it arrived. When I envisioned that dollar being yanked from that girl, I saw my hope being yanked away in the same manner. I began wallowing in my disappointment, and I unleashed my anger and bitterness upon the Lord.

Now friend, before I pour my transparent heart out to you, this is me being brave and vulnerable by putting this out for anyone in the world to read, so I hope you read this with grace and understanding. This dark moment would typically be something I would share only with my most intimate and trusted friends. However, because I believe that you and others may also struggle with where God is during a crisis. I am laying my genuine darkest moments out before you so that YOU can gain the same hope I have even if you have to struggle for it as I did. Here is the scene as I entered into those dark moments.

James and I were now dealing with Braylynn's second post-transplant hospital stay during Christmas weekend, the doctors were still trying to figure out why Braylynn was running a fever and our oldest son was back in crisis, but this time it was worse. James was persistently seeking out the Lord and our closest godly counsel to gain wisdom about how to handle Justin's situation while being over one hundred miles away.

James and I were also trying to navigate what felt like a betrayal committed by people who had been closest to us and we were discussing and praying how to work through it. We also just received news that one of the sweetest people we had ever encountered, who helped us keep hope during Braylynn's cancer battle, had lost her battle to cancer, which reminded us that this disease was still a battle Braylynn could lose. Last but not least, we were dealing with a mold issue in our house in Lafayette, which we had been trying to have fixed before Braylynn came home. My thoughts often drifted off to the Lord, and I would ask, "Lord, what more do you want from us?" I felt like we had no more to give.

What should have been the most wonderful time of the year was a whole lot of chaos for us. Amid the chaos in my life and my mind, God allowed me to bump into a momma in the parking garage who was also living in the Hog's House and who I had spoken to a bit during our time there. She was one of a few mommas that I had the privilege to talk and pray with during our time in New Orleans. All of us mommas at the Hog's House were going through heart-wrenching times with our children, which allowed us to occasionally connect.

This particular momma that I had bumped into in the parking garage had a newborn who recently had open heart surgery. She was struggling with how she was going to care for the baby, the newborn's twin and her toddler. I dug down deep within myself, and I encouraged her with the small bit of encouragement I had left inside of me. After I walked away from her, I could feel my spirit breaking apart as if it was leaving me, almost as if my breath was dissipating. All I could see at that moment was all the walls that were crumbling around us, and I could no longer give out hope to others when I did not have any hope myself.

I knew it was time for Jesus and me to have what the old folks call a "come to Jesus meeting." Y'all, I was hanging on to a thread of hope that was unraveling and about to snap, and this is where I was the most spiritually weak, but I was about to gain the most spiritual strength I ever had. I just did not know it yet.

James left me to myself for the day as I journaled, prayed, worshipped and reached out to my closest friends for prayer. I knew I was going into a long private battle with just me and God and I knew it would be a battle that I had not quite experienced before.

I began to question who God was and what his intentions for our lives were. I questioned why He was letting things happen to all the parents that were longing for their children to be healed or who were watching their children die as well as why he was allowing all of these things to happen to our family. Thinking of all of these things made me furious. Here is a real and raw excerpt from my journal on the day I call The Battle For Hope. My thoughts are a little chaotic because I was in such a dark place, but you will get an understanding of where I was in the moment.

"God, I don't understand why you allow people to suffer the way they do. Sometimes it makes me question your love, if you are real or if you are the God the Bible portrays. Yet, even through the questioning, I still choose to believe you love us, and this is not the life you want for your people. I choose to believe it is the sin and brokenness of the world that brings this tragedy upon us, but so often it is not our fault, yet we have to endure the pain because of others sin

and brokenness. It is not fair, and I wish this pain were not the case for us and others but just like Jesus, who took the punishment for everyone's sin, I know it was not fair for him either.

I accept this life, this lot you have chosen for us, but I don't like it, and I wish it were easier. However, I can also be thankful that it is not harder because I know it could be. Can you just give us a break in 2019? Can you keep James, myself and all of our children healthy? I am choosing to believe you are a God of miracles, and I know my requests are not selfish because I know you love us, and that is what you want for us. So I want to see you do these things Lord. You say you can do them, so show me!

Lord, I am fighting to continue to believe you are who you say you are. If you are who you say you are, then I need you to help me continue to believe because believing in you is what has made life worth living. If I don't believe in you, then life will be useless, but I don't want to blindly believe. I need to know like I know that you are who you say you are, and right now, life is not showing me that you are who I have always believed you to be. Help me out!"

Friend, this was not my finest hours in life, and I had more internal battles than this one, but it was my most honest hours. During this day of struggle, which lasted seven straight hours, James and my closest friends encouraged and prayed for me. They would send texts, a video chat, or call to be sure I was making it through okay. Man, I have some great people in my life. Get you some friends like this y'all!

Now, I do not know if you have ever been in this spot before but for me, a life without God is no life at all, and I needed him to reveal his true self so I could steady myself in him and continue to hope for the good things he had promised. Even though my husband, who is like Jesus with skin on, and my friends never quit encouraging me, I had to have this battle with God on my own because I knew that was the only way I would come back in a solid, unshakeable way.

At the end of the seven hours, I was exhausted mentally, physically and spiritually, but I felt like I was on my way back to hope. I would like to be able to tell you that the entire battle ended that day, but it did not. However, the major revelation I received from the Lord that day was, even though I doubted him, he never left me, and that was when my thread of hope was no longer unraveling. It was becoming stronger. In the weeks to come He would reveal himself to me in so many ways, and my hope was restored.

While reading back through my journal I noticed that I consistently said, "I choose to believe." My choice to believe is a literal representation of walking out what I preach and how I apply it when life is before me.

I have studied God's word for the majority of my life and I try to apply it in my life when I consciously can. Choosing to live out the words God breathed onto the pages of the Bible gave me the strength to walk in faith and obedience through the battle before me. It gave me the courage to not give up because of what I was feeling. Choosing to believe God when I do not see his truth is not easy, but it is necessary for me if I want to overcome anything I am facing.

Proverbs 13:12 tells us that, "Hope deferred makes the heart sick…" and I believe my heart had become very sick, which prompted my battle to gain back my hope.

This verse goes on to say, "…but a longing fulfilled is a tree of life." The Lord began to fulfill my longings when Braylynn was released from the hospital a second time, and we finally got to go home on Christmas Eve. We were able to spend Christmas with most of our children and grandchildren, which began to give life to my spirit and also open my heart back up to receive and hear God. Seeing my grandchildren in person that day filled my heart with warmth and I hoped for many happier days to come with them.

We also began dealing with the issues that were going on within our family. Our house was moving forward in its repairs. Braylynn's second bone marrow biopsy and test for Ph+ Chromosome came back negative and her body continued to show 100% donor cells for at least sixty days.

My life and my longings were being fulfilled. Little glimmers of hope were beginning to creep back in.

It still took me a couple of weeks of questioning and dealing head-on with all the issues we were facing to fully restore my faith in God and get back on my path of hope. And just as God does with me, one day in the middle of him turning the tide of all what we were facing, he spoke very clearly to me, and it was something I felt I had to share on our social media page also because I knew my struggles and my revelation would help someone else. Here is what God revealed to me and what I shared.

"Last night God gave me a perfect reminder of where he has been through this journey, even when I did not feel that he was there.

He was in every encouraging text, every phone call where someone checked on us, every card written by dear friends to encourage us, every meal cooked by someone else, every monetary donation, every Christmas gift, every visit from friends who drove all the way to New Orleans to be sure we did not feel alone, every blood donation in Braylynn's name, every daily encouraging video received from awesome friends, every prayer prayed for our family, all of our team who worked hard to keep our business going despite our absence, every hospital employee who cared for Braylynn, and us, and every person who asked, "How can I help?" God met us through Every. Single. Person. who cared for our family in any way!

When there are days of doubt: when the days look bleak: when you question if God is there because the circumstance is not ideal, look into the face of someone who is there listening and doing. That is God."

Even though I did not feel God throughout the dark days, I experienced him through the love of others, and that was God's way of continually giving me hope. But we were still in need of more hope as we continued because Braylynn's journey was not over.

Hang on to Hope

Chapter Twelve
THE DAY WE WERE HOPING FOR BUT NOT THE NEWS WE EXPECTED

. . . .

As we ventured into our final days and we began seeing things we hoped for come to fruition, my thoughts still wandered. I would think things like, "I wonder if Braylynn has a headache will it be just a headache, or when she has a cough will it be just a cough, or will a bruise just be a bruise? Could any of these instances mean her cancer is back? Will our family issues be resolved and relationships reconciled? Will the mold issues in our home be fixed promptly? When will we get to stop driving back and forth to New Orleans? When will life go back to normal?" In those times I had to remind myself, "God has not taken Braylynn, or us, this far only to go this far, and we are hanging on to hope that she is cured and our family will be whole again."

Thankfully, the doctor released us a month early, and we were able to go back home to Lafayette because Braylynn was doing so well, as long as we agreed to drive back twice a week for her appointments in New Orleans. We happily packed all our belongings and drove back home to Lafayette, and I was sure not sad to say goodbye to our tiny one-room room a month early!

All four of us were very excited to head home for good. I thought about how magnificent it would be to have our own space again at home. Brayden needed to be home more than any of us because he is so energetic, and the tiny space was not conducive for a twelve-year-old, active boy. I was particularly happy that he was going to get back to a more normal routine with friends, church and extra-curricular activities. But because our nearly weekly in and out of the hospital routine for the previous nine months had become normal, my heart still was not settled as we drove home. I was worried that we were not actually leaving behind our final hospital stay. However, I was hopeful that we would not return to the hospital and I tried to keep my focus on all the good things that awaited us at home.

Even though we were home Braylynn was not allowed to go outside, visit people or be in crowded places. We used the downtime to catch up on work and everything else that had been piling up while we were gone for two and a half months.

We waited for day +100 to arrive because the doctors told us that by that day, Braylynn's body should be better recovered from any sickness, and her immune system should start improving by leaps and bounds.

We finally arrived at day +100 on February 14, 2019. We started the day with pink cupcakes, and we made Braylynn a shirt to wear on her special day that read, "SCT

Survivor Post 100 Days!" We were ready to celebrate all day long! We left for a quick doctors appointment Braylynn had in New Orleans, and since she was feeling so well, we decided we would venture out to the zoo, which was a superb treat because she had not been outside except to walk to and from the car for three and a half months.

We had been recently informed that for the first year post-transplant that Braylynn was at risk of losing her stem cell engraftment if she was to get sick. Since we were aware of the risks, we made sure to be cautious and keep her as free from germs as possible. Of course, knowing the risks, it put this momma on heightened alert for germs. As we walked throughout the zoo, I frequently yelled, "Don't touch anything! Don't put your hands in your mouth, your nose or your eyes! Hand sanitizer!" Even with all the precautions, it was still the most fun, happiest day we had experienced in over nine months, and we all enjoyed it.

Braylynn especially enjoyed her time at the zoo. She laughed and played as she soaked up the sun, walked around outside without tubes or IV's stuck to her, and viewed all the animals in real life instead of watching them on T.V. from a hospital bed.

That is, until 4:00 pm during the car ride home when my cell phone rang, I answered, and the voice on the other line said, "Hello, this is the nurse from the doctor's office, I have the doctor on the line. Can you hang on please?"

You are probably thinking, "That certainly can't be good." Well, you are correct. The transplant doctor got on the phone and proceeded to tell me that Braylynn's most recent spinal tap showed Leukemia cells in her spine and that her spinal tap would need to be repeated in a few days to confirm the findings. I was devastated. Brayden and Braylynn were both in the car with James and me, and I certainly did not want to say anything in front of them yet. That made for a quiet last hour of our car ride home: I wanted Brayden and Braylynn to continue having the most fabulous day they had in months.

In that hour of silence, my thoughts were all over the place, and it was just God and me again. "God, why would you put Braylynn through all of this only to have Leukemia show up again? Was this all just a waste of time? Our entire family went through hell only to end up here?" It was taking a lot of strength for me to hold back the tears as we finished that car ride home.

Once we arrived home, James and I discussed what our next steps should be. We decided to call our pastors and a few of our trusted friends so they could pray with us.

When I spoke to one of my close friends she said, "I am going to remind you of what y'all have been standing on, and that is 'hang on to hope.'"

Don't you love when your friends quote you in your most significant time of need?

We decided that even though we had been very public with Braylynn's disease before that, we would keep this quiet and only in our close circle until we got more information and a better confirmation. Our spirit knew God was up to something here.

We prayed over Braylynn that night and asked God to remove the Leukemia cells from her spine. We agreed this was another opportunity to hang on to hope.

A few days later her spinal tap was repeated, and we did not receive a phone call, which was odd because after the spinal tap that showed Leukemia cells we received a phone call within forty-eight hours. I bet you are thinking, "No news is good news, right?" Well, you are correct again!

This time the results showed Atypical cells, which meant what the doctors thought were Leukemia cells were possibly diseased cells of an unknown origin, but not Leukemia cells. Having the Atypical cells was better because it could mean several non-harmful things could be happening in her spine, so we repeated the spinal tap in three weeks to confirm the results.

Three weeks later, her spinal tap had even better results. No diseased cells at all! What we had prayed and hoped for came to pass! This news was a massive relief and opened a new insight into what the future could be for Braylynn. We finally were able to cross over a bridge of belief that Braylynn would live out a normal childhood and experience lots of things most girls her age would experience.

The four of us began to settle back into our home in Lafayette. We all enjoyed the small amount of company we could have over while Braylynn's immune system continued to build up. James, myself and Brayden were thrilled to attend church again, and even though James and I had to switch out our church attendance so one of us could stay home with Braylynn, it was comforting to return to what had been our church home for nearly two decades. We also enjoyed sitting on our porch and getting to visit with our neighbors and seeing our grandchildren face to face instead of via FaceTime.

We felt like life was getting somewhat back to normal when our next hope-filled surprise came a few weeks later when James received a phone call from Justin. He called James to let him know that he was working to renew his life, and that he was in a sustainable place and reconciling relationships. It just so happened that Hali had a birthday coming up, and it was an excellent opportunity for all of our children and grandchildren to come together. We planned a sweet birthday breakfast for all of us to celebrate, and we were expecting great things!

It had been far too long since we could all celebrate together, when our children were not sick or in a crisis. We were all stronger, we were all in a healthier place and I felt that day we celebrated Hali's birthday all together was the best day we ever had in the entire nineteen years we had been together as a family. Our hope finally came to fruition.

Hang on to Hope

Chapter Thirteen
WHAT WOULD HAPPEN IF THE OUTCOME HAD BEEN DIFFERENT?

. . . .

I am fully aware that all stories do not end the way ours has. Not all adult children get through their crisis, not all children survive cancer, reconciliation does not happen for all marriages and families and not everything works out the way we plan it. That includes Braylynn's journey with cancer: chemo and stem cell transplants can create several other issues in the body, so she will be monitored regularly for the rest of her life. When things have not quite worked out yet it gives us another opportunity to hang on to hope. Our other children may develop some new crisis or reveal unresolved issues of their own, but you know what? We will hang on to hope.

There were so many times during this journey that James and I said out loud that we would hang on to hope out of complete obedience. I often had conversations with God about how we would still have hope if one of our children did not survive their crisis, but I know that ultimately our hope was not just in our children's healing, or the healing of our family. Our hope was in God. James and I had many discussions that included the words, "Even if the healing is not seen here on earth, our hope comes in who He is, not in the plan we think is supposed to happen."

Choosing to hang on to hope means that holding on to hope, by faith and through our pain, can and will give hope to someone else. Choosing to hang on to hope can inspire another child going through a tough time to be brave like Braylynn. Choosing to hang on to hope can encourage other parents of struggling children to continue believing in a miracle for their child. Choosing to hang on to hope is choosing to believe that even if Braylynn's disease returns or if another crisis happens within our other children or ourselves, we know God will never leave us and that we will come out stronger on the other side. Choosing to hang on to hope is choosing to hang on to Him because he is our Hope.

WANT MORE INFO?

If you would like to view our journey of hanging on to hope you can search the hashtag #HangOnToHope and visit our FB page at **https://www.facebook.com/james.bertrand1**. You can message us or send us a friend request. We would love to hear how our story inspired you to hang on to hope in your journey.

Also, if you would like to find out more about adoption or foster care in the United States, visit **https://adoptuskids.org/**

About the Author

Candy loves Jesus with all her heart. She lives in Lafayette, La. with her husband James, who she adores more than any other human being in the world. Candy is finishing out her parenting years raising the last two of five children, who her and James have co-parented together, and enjoying their three grandchildren.

When Candy is not tending to the needs of her home you can find her ministering to women who have walked through pain and encouraging them with the same hope that she found in Jesus.

Although Candy does not have a love for writing she is now a self-published author and hopes her words of hope bring healing to those in need. You can find her on Instagram under **candyggb** where she most likely is drooling over videos of dogs doing all sorts of cute things.

Hang on to Hope

Hang on to Hope

Hang on to Hope

77509397R00057

Made in the
USA
Columbia, SC